# Kissing DARKNESS

## Love Poems & Art

### CAROLYN MARY KLEEFELD
### DAVID WAYNE DUNN

Inquiries about *Kissing Darkness* should be addressed to:

RiverWood Books
PO Box 3400
Ashland, Oregon 97520 USA
www.riverwoodbooks.com

Inquiries about the authors' artwork, fine art cards and other books
should be addressed to:

Atoms Mirror Atoms, Inc.
PO Box 221693
Carmel, California 93922 USA
(800) 403-3635
(831) 667-2433
www.carolynmarykleefeld.com

Design by MaddoxDesign.net
Cover: "Union with the Muse", Oil/Canvas 24" x 18"
by Carolyn Mary Kleefeld.
Front flap: Detail from "Midnight Kiss", Oil/Canvas 20" x 16"
by Carolyn Mary Kleefeld.
Authors' Photograph: Ronna Emmons

First Printing 2003

Printed in Indonesia

ISBN:1-883991-83-8

# CONTENTS

## Carolyn Mary Kleefeld

## David Wayne Dunn

## Carolyn Mary Kleefeld

## David Wayne Dunn

# CONTENTS

## Carolyn Mary Kleefeld

## David Wayne Dunn

## Carolyn Mary Kleefeld

## David Wayne Dunn

# PAINTINGS

# DEDICATIONS

DEEP GRATITUDE TO:

David Wayne Dunn, the fearless chameleon-muse of these love songs, who continues to kiss the darkness with me as a way of life.

And to Patricia Holt, the godmother of this work, who contained within her, every line of this verse in its birthing stages – and with exquisite editorial attunement, sublime dedication, patience and undaunted fortitude made this book possible.

Also to Kirtana, Wild Dove, the other godmother of this book, my abiding appreciation for her caring editorial assistance, endless patience, dedication and supreme organization, who also made this book possible.

For dearest Carla Kleefeld, my treasured blessing, with whom I share ancient origin and most sacred, inspired rapport.

To Steven Scholl, deep gratitude for his confidence in this book and for making its publication possible.

For Judie Najarian, special appreciation for all of her supreme generosity and valued assistance.

With appreciation for Mytheos Holt, who at fourteen years old has an ancient soul that understands what creation requires.

Special thanks for their support and assistance to:
Linda Van Allan, Ronna Emmons, Celeste Worl, Kay Walters, Gail Bengard, Marla Bell and Birgit Maddox.


*Carolyn Mary Kleefeld*

For Carolyn, darling Lover of my dreams –
To say more than what is
within these pages: thank you

For their patient sensitivity
toward my life and my soul,
I dedicate these songs to
Patricia and Mytheos Holt

Special thank yous to Kirtana,
Carla Kleefeld, Celeste Worl, Steven Scholl,
Linda Van Allen, Cynthia Dunn,
Ray Holland and Judie Najarian

Prayers and love to my mother,
whose strength and courage feed
me throughout my days

And to the currents of life
that tear apart and draw together,
I bow.

*David Wayne Dunn*

# FOREWORD

*Kissing Darkness* takes us into the evolving world, at once ethereal and earthly, of the lovers – first, as they yield to their passion; then, as they confront the dark world of mortality and suffering which threatens their relationship. From this dark world they find their way to a love that sustains and nourishes them. The story of their journey, told in individually and collaboratively written poems, is distinctly personal and universal. In taking us to 'this abundant moment,' this 'breathless garden' of their love, Carolyn and David provide a testament to love's healing grace.

– *Elliot Ruchowitz-Roberts*
Co-author, *"Bowing to Receive the Mountain"*
Co-editor/co-translator, two works from the *"Telugu"*
Co-editor, the college text *"Bridges"*

*I close the door;*

*your love opens it.*


*I close the door again;*

*your love removes the hinges.*


**David Wayne Dunn**

*The Immortal Lovers*

## DAVID'S LETTER

Your letter ignited
the savage pain
of love's touch,
arousing my numbed passions
sleeping as drugged beasts
hiding from life behind masks

The fruits of passion were lost
to repetitious themes,
nailed to the habits of time

Your words planted seeds
in my desert within

# UNION AWAITING ME

I see through the mists
of the departing storms,
your face coming
forward to touch

Your dark maleness
travels the wind,
settling in my every crevice,
promising the intimacy
lost to barren-heartedness,
lost to decay,
the corrosion of time

Dare I dream of
a love so grand
that lament just feeds
as the winter's rain,
our love to flourish?

You may be a phantom
instead of a dream to be

It matters not,
as you've shown me,
even in your absence,
the union awaiting me

# I SAY NOTHING

I say nothing tonight
so as not to commit blasphemy

I say nothing tonight
as words cannot speak
of what you live in me

I say nothing tonight
because when you depart,
you are closer than ever

I say nothing tonight
as the stars pour from your eyes,
blossoming constellations within

I say nothing tonight of this night
as I crawl between my pink sheets
beholding forever your entrance
into my heart, my life, my eternity

I say nothing tonight,
because what is felt must
have its freedom from words
that dare attempt constraint
of our wingéd glory

# WITH A COMPANION

Ah, I travel at last with a companion
who knows what it means to get lost

We travel into the depths of earth
and soar with the angels' wings

Ah, I travel at last with a companion
who knows what it means
to give oneself up – to More,
that dying is the fruit of love
and love the seed of eternal death

Ah, I travel at last with a companion
who goes with me through portals
of raging cities and out again,
wandering the transparent worlds

# BEARING THE WHITE FACE OF GOD

O, dearest one, do you know
you are an instrument
of God's music, so divine?

Do you know He lives through you,
although not you alone?

In your extravagance of soul,
you allow yourself unmercifully
both the torments of living death
and the boundless song of love...

Endlessly becoming the newborn lily
in the eternal meadows,
bearing the white face of God...

Letting yourself be the Aeolean harp
on which the Elements
play their greater existence

O, dearest one, do you know
the gems of your royal necklace
are poems manifesting through you?

# RESTS THE SLEEPING BIRD

How to speak
of the gods and the ages
How to wander
the pulse of the earth

Within your voice,
a stillness lingers
Within your sound,
rests the sleeping bird

I lie back, letting your roots
reach into mine,
feeling your wings envelop me
in a fluttering tenderness

In the fresh, falling dew
of autumnal night,
I see your face
in the glistening leaves of a tree,
in the longing for light

As a star clinging
to the ebony dome,
you emerge, enlustered
with the splendor born
of the deepest heart

# O LUNAR LANTERN OF THE NIGHT

O lunar lantern of the night,
your crescent casts shimmering beams
upon the body of your mistress sea

Your cold fire haunts the trees,
enters the bedroom
riding crystal beads,
nestles in our embracing bodies,
feeding our love, lunar wine

I imbibe your silvery pollen,
drinking of us, my beloved and I,
and of the blue wisteria bloom

The roses red, flower quickly
from my lover's chest,
from the orchards
of his burgeoning ravines

Intoxicated, we stumble on,
falling to sleep
on evening's quiet hammock

## ALLOW THIS ISLE TO BE

Standing in the forest,
drinking in the vast sweetness,
the balm of silence,
the most seductive of gods,
I reach out with abandon
to seek that bottomless well of union –
elated, yet quietly so,
wearing transparent veils,
the non-colors of nature's silence

I come to thee,
my lord of dusk,
with your arms of amber hue
and gems of ruby red
adorning your leonine chest

Yes, and how I come to you,
dressed in an invisible balm,
in the gossamer of lavender moonlight
cloaking the white stones

You are there,
hidden in the wind-stirred leaves
In that music of the wilds,
you thrive

I join you in this soundless music
born of you, I and the gods
who finally allow this isle, to be

# THE KIND GODS OF WINTER

The long, pale fingertips of winter
play their raindrops across the cabin's roof,
haiku bells from ancient worlds resounding

This untamed melody ebbs and flows,
pulsing of the heavens' fulfilled desire

The pink hyacinth blooms,
enraptured from the rain's pulse
Petals dance beyond their stem
before our astonished eyes

At last the wind-beast slithers away
Somber, saturated, he flees
to boundaries unknown
Everywhere is soaked and shaken
in the storm's frenzied arms

And here within,
we nestle by the blazing fire,
covered by a leopard-spotted wrap
Animal creatures are we,
glowing within the cabin's coziness

And the velvet muzzle of deer nearby
hiding in the wet thicket –
do they know this comfort,
sometimes born to you and I?

In my soul, the raindrops echo,
water chimes chanting
through my every pore,
resounding a sacred rhythm
from heaven's shore,
a mantra gently moving
the forest to verse

*continued*

Do the deer hear this?
The great lions in their prowl?

Ah, for once to be human
holds such grace –
to be chosen for this
symphonic blossoming of ear,
is to be wreathed
by the kind gods of winter

# ANCIENT GODDESS LIGHT

O luminous flower, waning,
visage enshrouded by passing mists,
your world is suspended
in sovereign glory,
crowned by a halo of rosette hue

You cast a glittering path
across the writhing sea,
shimmering up our streams
as we behold your prayer in silence

Our love shines resplendent
in your ancient goddess light
In the infinity of skies and seas,
we become you, one dream

O illumining vessel,
as the clouds obscure you,
we become, like you, invisible

# YOUR QUIET GODLINESS

In the quiet of your godliness,
can you know the thrust
of your spirit's flame
gave me the eyes to behold,
the ears to imbibe
the orchestration of the tides?

In the quiet of your godliness,
can you know the pines
standing so silently tall
murmur from their roots into mine?

Your quiet godliness touches me
with a creature's pulse,
as deeply as the songs
of the whispering stream
soothe my soul

Can you know the thrust
of your spirit's flame
has emblazoned my senses
to unknown rhapsody?

In the quiet of your godliness,
can you know?

*Untitled*

## MY MOST HOLY DEAR

Know that in silence
I am speaking to you.
Know that in silence my soul
rings out like a light to you.
Know that every whispering branch
on the tree of life is my breath
whispering for you.

Blow through me,
my eternal wind. Blow through me,
my eternal mistress, ...or "my eternal love harvest"
my most holy dear.
Blow through me.
Leave not one clothed leaf
wavering on my vibrating stem.

# FROM THE SACRED URGES

I saw the black clouds
of sorrow and desire fall
like stones from the sky,
breaking the black back
of the remorseful sea.

I felt then
the old rotting spines
of longing dissolve.
I felt then
the new bones being born
from the sacred urges.

(Her marrow even manifested
itself before my eyes!)

I felt then:
You are totally mad!
I felt then,
the love of her touch.

## LOVE POEM

What skies
have fallen softly
to lay white stars
upon your shoulders?

Half asleep
between pink sheets
I reach for you
and wonder –

What sacred god of living flesh
hath formed you with such splendor?

And do you feel
how with our touch,
the already vast night increases –
all the stars falling
to become a single rose.

# THE DISTANCES

I could proclaim
without shame
like streaming stars in the night sky –
your existence.
I could surround you
with prayer, or with nothingness,
that would become you.
I could dream
about secret gardens.
You would appear,
but not until midnight,
not until the moon
had risen to meet
the pollen of white jasmine,
would you appear.
I would open my eyes
and my soul would hold you
in its gaze.

Stars we will always share.
And the light-leaves
dancing in the meadows
like green bells.

Distances we share.
Unknowable, of course
unspeakable,
the distances.

# A THOUSAND RUBIES

There are a thousand rubies
in one mine, yet we're seeking
gold everywhere.

Instead of diamonds, lovers prefer
the poetry of midnight, promising roses
and promising dawns.

When I dream of you, tear-filled
rivers flow in my heart –

And all the flowers,
too delicate to behold,
look like naked souls.

# HAND WITHIN HAND

I know there exist
rivers...

Quiet places where
the river and dawn
walk side by side
hand within hand
under lavender skies.

And I know a place
not far from here
where solitude deepens,
where giant oak trees
lay fallen in still meadows
like giants on their knees –

The blaring death-wind
of winter still echoes
in their hollows.

I go there
on my own knees sometimes
to watch the new green
emerge from the thick trunks.

The flame
of the future lives
in that green; the soul
of the world grows and
changes; life grows
and the flesh of trees falls;
life's urge is renewed
and destroyed in every moment.

Existence moves toward
what future I do not know
and vow never to care.

## ONE NIGHT OR A THOUSAND NIGHTS

Dream me
like a prayer
held for a moment
in your hands.

Or think of me
as a tree
whose roots drink
from your river-soul.

Please, stop all these
black-crow thoughts,
and let me be
a star somewhere
in your deepest night.

# I WANT TO WALK WITH YOU

I want to walk
with you at night
enveloped by the mystery
of the holy dark.
I want to stroll with you
under skies too rich with stars
to ever be possessed.
I want not to own a single star –
only embrace them all,
then give them away –
let them fall through my hands
to your waiting eyes.

## LOVE SONG

Where are you?
Are you sleeping now
or are you waking?

Where are your hands?
Where are your lips,
your arms?

Are you here?
Is anything really ever here?

Are you mine?
Tell me.
Do you know?
Tell me.

Where are your eyes?
What are you wearing?
What soft thing falls
to your flesh like the
breath of a rose?

What necklace today
is so fortunate
to be worn by you –
what sparkling gems
are laughing at their good luck?

Where are you now?
Are you wearing your hair up,
or is it down?

(O blessed shoulders!)

Do you know I am here,
with you?

*continued*

## LOVE SONG *continued*

Do you feel my love, my love?
Do you share my freedom?

Is that your hand on me?
The flesh too, is a spirit –
and yours is like dripping flowers.

Every line, every form
of your flashing beauty,
every shadow of shadow
that forms your face,
every birthing light...

Do you know I adore?
Do you know I enter every
part of you when you slumber
and when you wake?
(Do you know I am touching you now?)

Do you feel me?
Is every cell that bears you
bearing my light, my love?

Are the atoms of your flesh
dancing with joy?

Do you know I adore?
Do you care?
Tell me.

There is not an animal
or an angel in all the kingdoms
thirsting more than my blood for you.

Let me kiss you.
(Do you think poets kiss differently?)

*continued*

*DWD*

Are you smiling,
dear one? Or are
your lips parted
with goodbye, like
the lovers of red dawns?

Come, let me touch you.
Let me find the place
that has never been known
by either of us.

Let me kiss you there.

Let me place upon you
more than my hands,
more than my lips,
my blood.

*Love Dream of Spring*

# SONG TO DAVID

To bear such love
I am on my knees
As the humble willow tree
bends in the storm,
I bow to the wildest force
that ever so consumed me

Such beauty only the angels glimpse,
yet a terror rises like a fierce wave,
threatening to overwhelm me

In the yielding to such splendor,
my gardens grow wild,
tall grasses of verdant green,
turning crimson in autumn's last leaf

My blood races in the storm,
holding close your pulse
in the glory of a passion
so deeply rooted,
it humbles me in its gentle touch

# WHEN I SING TO YOU

Ah, when I sing to you,
why is it the gods answer?

When I sing to you,
the roots of trees
rustle their dried leaves,
murmur into my deeper streams

And you, too, soar,
riding the backs of flying panthers
Glossy angels with fiery eyes
lead our song-bursts
with feathered torch

Ah, when we are singing,
the silhouettes of trees blacken
against the reddened cheeks of sundown

Is the song I sing to thee
an ancient rhythm
resounding from the past,
calling us beyond the hands of time,
encouraging the angels of tomorrow
to lend their wings, kiss us,
and guide us on

# DRINKING OF THE UNION SO FLEETING

After the storm,
the midnight sky
looms bold, black, primal –
raw without desire,
ready to be eaten
by our hungry souls

And today,
after the endless rain
that dashed the petals away,
the earth is rich with
the tempest's charge,
its rivers proud again,
joining the sea

And I, beloved,
how I melt into our nakedness,
drinking of the union so fleeting

# THE WIND MOANS FOR THE LOVER'S LOVE

The slashing tongue
of the wind-beast howls,
encircling the small redwood nest
amidst the snow-capped mountain peaks
Angrily, he demands to play,
dashing, thrashing sheets of rain
across the windowpane

The lovers, hidden in each other's flesh,
ignore the wild, wet beast outside

The wind howls on alone,
lost in this wilderness
of massive mountains tumbling
to the fathomless seas below

Within their rustic haven,
the lovers hungrily devour
each other's passion

The candles' flames dance
as chords in this Dionysian fugue,
heralding their sacred, erotic bed
Colors rich as a Persian carpet
unthread from their golden fiber,
feathering flights for their flocked wings

Jeweled necklaces emerge,
adorning their necks –
red and orange, pinks and corals
of their spilt desire,
borne of the winter's storm

She breathes the dusky smoke
of her heart's flames
into his madrone of tree

*continued*

*CMK*

A fragrance thickens
from whence it came,
moistening their flowing silks of skin

A heated essence floods their chamber,
murmuring of the creatures' play
Mangoes ripen in their touch,
incensed beyond a mortal's word

And the wind grows fainter,
for the moment, echoing
in the lower ravines, rejected still,
moaning, crying for the lover's love

# LIE UPON YOUR PATH

The blood of the garnet's tear
bathes in the moon's pale sheen
as I lay myself upon the earth,
a slave of love's madness

You may not see me there
lying on your path,
but if you do, lie beside me
and cover me with kisses

Let the blood of your garnet's tear
bathe with mine
in the moon's cool embrace,
as we recline on the heavens' shores
and grow from the stars
mirrored in our eyes

The ebony of night will soothe us,
and the dawn mend our wounds

Yes, my darling,
let me lie upon your path,
with you next to me,
receiving the heavens in our hearts,
illumined in our marrow

# THE DEATH THAT HOLDS THE TORCH

Here I am, so filled with you,
with the earth's fecundity
amidst the amber of autumn's hue

Yet in my passion for you,
in its thirsting fervor,
I always yearn for you
as the moth to the flame,
the drawing into oblivion,
the wanting that is dying,
the giving up of self to More,
the death that holds
the torch for life's embrace

*Untitled*

# SOMEDAY YOU'LL TURN THE LAST PAGE

Someday you'll turn
the last page of your book of life
and read no more
the starry story of your dreams.

Someday you'll move
with such grace, you'll be invisible.

Someday you'll be gone
but the grass you walked
on will remain and sing
like poets from the soil.

Someday you'll never see flowers again,
never kiss the soft petals,
never touch the tender leaves.

Someday you'll be dead,
but it won't feel like forever to anyone;
you'll live in the breasts of birds and men
like music that is pregnant
and wants to be born.

Someday, visions and dreams and life
and death are all going to be married
(if they aren't already)
and you'll be where you've always been –
here, within me.

# THE NAKED DEATH

This fleeting life.
This transient, ever-changing world.
Time and no time, again,
look what falls from my shoulders;
my hands cannot grasp understanding.
When fear comes again to me,
come to me, my king of silence,
my lord of the moon.
Pierce my shut heart where
every dark root grows.
There, beside the bitter boulders
of my being, release me from
this prison. Plant instead
a few seeds of mercy; move
the stones of solitude
that bruise me so deceptively.
Why should I shudder for you?
Dear is the autumn twilight.
Dear the fragrance of my tears.
I who would linger forever
now linger on.
Show me, my prince of spring,
what it is like when the white
morning opens and rises
from your breath.
Never leave me.
Show me what every April
promises and every August fulfills.
Laugh at me, naked in your garden.
Sustain me, bright one, or else lose
your way with me; lead me
to my destination.
Let every leaf fall
and the naked death of a lover
still proclaim you.

## THIS LIFE

Tell them that we celebrated
experience until it made us sick.

Tell them that we sang songs
until the dawn, and not always joyfully.

Tell them even our sorrows
were magical and every pain
somehow a blessing.

Tell them that we loved
even while we lost and,
losing, we gained the
whole world.

## OVERTURE

To live and to be broken.
To live and to be torn – open.

Ah to live.
Ah to open and to live and to be
broken again and again until
what most destroys us becomes us
and we are naked again.

Our sorrow becomes song.

## NOW THAT I AM NAKED

Now that I am naked.
Now that I have been exposed
to pain and suffering and madness –
do you love me more?
Now that my wounds have been seen
and the people stare,
do you hold me closer?

This morning, on white stones
in the sunlight,
I removed my clothing.
I laid myself bare
and felt my fingers bruised.
Do painful hands hold you nearer?
Is anguish and separation your sister?
Do you like it when I cry?
Do you exult when hope is missing?
Why do passing clouds,
like fleeting pleasure,
please you so much?
Shall I make you poems?
Must I speak openly of my soul?

Down the mountain slope,
there were four brown deer among
the brown leaves of winter.
What about their souls, lord, when
the season of April is born
and desire violently fills them?
What is harmony, then, lord,
when desire is often only like a fear
that drives us to extremes?

Now that I am naked...

## WHEN I AM DYING

When I'm dying,
tell me about a secret place
where the river flows
and the dawn rises
quietly over the mountains
with pink lips
kissing my soul.

When I'm dying,
lead me down the river
through the passage of dreams.

When I'm dying,
show me your hands
one more time;
then touch me
as softly as you can,
like the breath
of a prayer falling
from me to you.

## UNTITLED LAMENT

You used to come in the morning.
Do you remember?
Now, after many long days of silent
suffering, you show your face again.
I remember.
And if I reach out too eagerly for you,
don't retreat, do not run away.
It is only that I have missed you
and still desire you to be nearer, nearer.
So come, come close my darling
and tell me what a fool I've been that
I did not bow lower in your absence.
Tell me that my patience needs yet
to be born and my soul, if it is to
survive, must learn to be still.
O solitude. O aloneness.
Why is it that your pleasures are always
laced with bittersweetness? And how far
do I have yet to travel to return to that
place where solitude is sweet again?
O how far?

## ALMOST UNBEARABLE

Life is so hard
(for so many)
I am too soft.

My heart,
my mind,
my body.

One flower falling
from your hair
sends me reeling.

I stumble down
the long stairway to
the bottomless pit
of never-forgotten
dreams.

What I find there
is an even deeper love,
almost unbearable.

# NO BITTER GOD SHALL TASTE US

The wine whispered
to the wine glass,
"Open, open, let me pour
my sweetness into you;
let the rich color of my being
blend with the transparency
of your glass; let the glass
and the wine become indistinguishable,
and no bitter god shall taste us."

## LAMENT

Sometimes
I need to touch
candlelight,
not the light
that loves
from your eyes.

Sometimes
the wind calls me
when you call me
and I die between
callings.
How can I be
all these answers?

## I AM ON MY KNEES

If life
is what brings me
to my knees, O love,
so it must be;
I am on my knees.
But also: let my longing
sing of you, cry out
if need be... (I am
crying out) about your
utter delicacy.

And those flames
that rise from earth
as flowers,
they too shine for only a
moment in brilliant
harmony –
only to die, only to die...

From shattered hulls
of holy seeds under sighing soil,
what brought forth
the blossom but the birth
and the necessity
of unfolding opposites?

Ah, dancing light merging
with the still, whispering dark.

*Moon Angels*

# O ANGEL SOUL

How long, dearest soul,
have you lived
in those empty shadows
awaiting the long fingers
of the sun's beams to reach you?

How long, dearest soul,
have you wailed into
the catacombs of primordial night
awaiting an echo, perhaps
from a passing angel or ghost?

How long, shivering soul,
since you've felt complete?

How does it feel
to see the white, downy feather
fall at your feet?

How long has it been
since you've kissed
without death's desire
breathing alternately?

O angel soul,
perhaps it is you
who have birthed
your soul's echo in answer

# IN THE SOULS THAT SUFFER

Is it a poverty of soul
that climbs me up the mountain –
an ill-fitting malaise
sculpting its face in stone?

Yet, how you pour into me
the blood of your riches,
the red sunflower of your heart
offering the pale musk
of autumn's final fragrance

O spirit who loves in injury,
must such abundance
have the tinge of a wayward torture?

Hold me close, my dearest;
the wick of night stays lit
in the souls that suffer

# IN YOUR SEASONS

Do not fear for me, tender soul;
as with the rose on the mountaintop
which has borne the frost of winter,
spring has come each year and will again

Am I the one you fear for?
Or is it you?
Can we tell each other apart
when tenderness is so budding?

Yes, the winter has bitten my core;
the spring has embraced it
And you, in your seasons, do the same

## LOVE'S LIGHTNING

Stripped bare
of all but our essence,
we reveal our inner core

Now in our nakedness,
we tenderly touch,
behold the intimacy
that is ours to bear,
imbibe the fragrance
of our unfolding petals,
standing strong in the pain
of our injured beauty,
brave to the piercing bolt
of love's lightning

*CMK*

# THE DRAGON SINGS; THE DRAGON DIES

Last evening,
with the black trees towering
and the stars falling behind you,
you sang the nomad's lament
into the moonless night

Spanish gypsy music rode the tides
And lost, vanishing worlds echoed you

Today you reappear,
but the stars are gone
from your shoulders
The heavens have sunk
into your pain-soaked earth;
you've become the murky smoke
of a suffering reptile

I leave with unseeing eyes,
a numb senselessness,
a questioning soul

The dragon sings; the dragon dies –
in One breath, I muse

## TO THE CHILD OF DAWN

In being nothingness,
I may have emptiness,
and then perhaps winter's seed
may lodge quietly, veiled,
its fecund core in rest

Spring whispers with encouragement,
*"Come, come; do not fear.*
*Bear winter's fury.*
*Keep trusting the river's flow,*
*the exultant skies of voluminous clouds,*
*their islands of bathed stars*
*orbiting the celestial seas.*

*Bear it, bear it all,*
*white child of the dawn.*
*See the possibility born from passion.*
*Open the views of your windows.*

*No matter how ruthless the clime,*
*trust and you will see the blue balm of light*
*will shine in its own time,*
*which becomes your time*
*when you become one of life's flowers*
*with all the powers and vulnerabilities,*
*facing the winter of forces yet to come."*

And how was it, dear one,
living on the mountaintop
during the last wild storm?
Did you realize its seductive power,
its contradictory winds, as your own?

Or did you forget
and think it all your own myth,
dismissing the effects of the cosmic wave?

*continued*

Why live on a mountaintop
and subject your sensitivities
to such weather,
I ask the delicate child of dawn
Does the tiniest bird
find shelter amidst the turbulence?
Does the butterfly find a secret refuge?
Can we, as the tender ones,
find our mysterious lodging
in the nest of our dream's abode?

Yes, winter lies ahead,
but if our hearts are shining,
the garden still flourishes
as light, ever shed

Your love reaches me
as eternal pollination,
impregnating me with the gems
of your heart's pure gold

Ah, white child of the dawn,
I join you in this dance of forces,
smiling to the emerald whispers
of future's passing moments

# IN ANONYMITY

Here, on the vast summits
of endless mountain ranges –
here, where relentless winds
cry of life's insatiable longing,
my wings lie folded,
trying to soothe my spirit's sleep,
to comfort the dormant soul
of my vague heart

Obscured by heavy grayness,
tenuous, resting in amorphism,
I await the I of me
as the next cloud to be

The wind thrashes with shrilling voice,
moans at a lack of companions
The tiny bird of me, hidden,
avoids his longing grasps

Under the spell of imminent spring,
the dewdrop glistens,
an ephemeral sparkle within eternity

Lupines and wildflowers,
tiny in their unfolded faces,
hold the spring's secret
in their hidden wombs

Will they wreathe their erotic
fragrance around us soon?
Will the perfume
of our struggling love, so grand,
blend with theirs, again?

The force of life's great gales
sweeps through us with no remorse

*continued*

*CMK*

and little care, it appears,
yet fills us with the sun-god's meadows,
blossoming waves of wildflowers waltzing

And now today,
high upon the mountain's peak,
within our bold, redwood cabin,
we sequester, shunning the tearing storm,
wondering what lies within
those mad gusts of wind,
besides the pollen, so spread

Where next will my formless
and wandering soul climb?

The torpid envelope of gray has sealed us
in this exploring inquiry of worlds,
and the wind's wild bolero of longing
tempts not our dance, today

We are turned back within,
like the dormant seed, seeking refuge
and chance in anonymity

# A BLACK CROW FLIES

Over the dark blue desert dawn
a black crow flies
and a shadow falls
from my wingéd soul
onto the timeless boulders,
into the seams of
the darkest rock
where no frog can lie

There in the pristine
formlessness of dawn,
touched only by
the moon's diaphanous veil,
an emerald seed awaits
the unknown spring

# I WANDER THE GREEN

Tonight I feel the burgeoning
of green love again
The meadows of a crimson spring
breathe into the receding
bite of winter's cold,
as the white sun of your lambent heat
lingers in the shadows
of tomorrow's verdant bud

In the dawn's glistening dew
of rapture, your touch ignites
glowing embers of chance,
drinking of the vintage
of the tear's well of sorrow

The ashes, gray in the hearth
of my worn soul's fire,
are blown to oblivion

Naked and translucent,
I wander the green with you,
my cherished one
Here in the flesh,
raw to your touch, I am yours
as the forest embraces
its trees, eternally

*Untitled*

# DIARY

Today
I found a place
in nature's lap
where the sky opened
lovely arms and announced
emergence –
spring – love,
and the soft-petaled
palms of her upturned
hands spread like lords,
the flight of many graces.

I knelt on white knees
before hers,
incredible dawns
of emerging light
as resurrection drew near.

# FRAGMENTS FROM THE SHIP OF MY SOUL

What anchor needs
to be lifted from the ship
of my soul that it may sail
to you on the clearest waters
of love's understanding?

One gesture of one petal
from your many-flowered garden
is too much for me...

How many flowers
on your already burgeoning vine,
and still how utterly tenderly
you grow me one, this morning –
from the seed of my deepest fruit,
naked from your soul.

As if in towers high above grief,
the stars echo like holy lords...

May I become love more through you,
not to bear weight against you
but to gain myself while losing
myself – for you?

From all the stars, one love.
From the skies of the mind flowing,
one peace.
No clouds, but an endless
splendor of sky –

Stars like love,
and behind the stars,
immortal night –
and behind the immortal
night, You.

## "WHERE DO YOU GET THE INSPIRATION FOR YOUR POETRY?"

Your face mostly,
solitude in the morning
and white stones under
moonlight on dark hills.
Thoughtless animals
in the midnight forest.
The blood that moves them
and the blood that flows
through your hands.
My blood. My longing
for something that lasts.
My dark and light being
alternating with the world
like a wave in the sea.
The sea.
The unknowable depths
of the spirit of the world,
and trees.

# HOLY

Across her face
a shadow fell when
with tender hand she
delicately lit a candle.

And her hair from
the dancing shadows
looked like a mountain
of flowing ferns.

She sat beside me,
placing the candle between us,
and spoke softly:

"Pain," she said,
"is the shaping stone
that the waters
of our hearts
flow over;"

"Love is the flower
of night
hung between
sacred dawns;"

"God,"
she whispered lower,
"God is whatever you desire."

Moved to silence
I mindlessly reached
to touch her hand;
in my heart
something was echoing –
some subtle reverberation
like a flashing

*continued*

of falling feathers...

She stopped me
with questions,
but did not withdraw her hand.

"What are you doing?"
And then over
the yellow light:
"Why do you want
to touch my hand?"

I reached for her face
instead and said,

"It is my desire."

With smiling eyes
like mirrored stars,
she breathed: "Why, are you
making a God of me!"

"Wouldn't that be wrong?"
I asked, not really wanting
an answer.

"But I need
to tell you,
dare I tell you –
your beauty, to me,
is holy."

She laughed with
flowering pupils.
"Well, whatever
you desire!"

*continued*

"So touch me.
Yes, do touch me."

Then she looked
in a mirror.
"My shoulders,
are they not lovely,
dressed with
the flickering
candlelight?"

I reached
for them as if
reaching for the
secrets of life.

"Like little bridges
over paradise,"
I told her.
"Holy. Holy."

## WONDER WEARS NO CLOTHES

Wonder wears no clothes.
It is how I remember her the most.
Nakedly, her hands obsess me.
Nakedly, her soul haunts me.
By her beauty, I am taken
to another world. Or by her
love, this world is transformed.

It is true she makes me a fool.
It is appropriate that sometimes
I wear the color blue.

How I wish she were here now
and that other-worldly music were
pouring from her lips.

## LITTLE FLOWER

Little flower,
what are you doing?
Are you not yet held
by the lovely arms of summer
and still how secretly you come
to me with flirtatious eye
and painted petals, which
draw me to your ways.
How dare you!
Still I hold you fast.
(I am without shame)
I am not the sun that feeds you
nor the wind that scatters your
seeds. I am only a man, little
flower. A man you don't
even know. A man who
caresses you and adores you
more than men.

# WHILE WE ARE HUMAN

I never said I was enlightened.
I am suffering for the
mortal you. I cannot
save you for eternity;
I need you now,
I want you here.
– Not infinitely,
not metaphysically
but humanly, humbly.

I am not a Buddhist.
For I have an intricate,
complex, worldly
desire for you
and I am hopelessly
attached to the way
you appear, the way
you feel, the way
you smell.

I am not a king, but women
have had me. Now I am
no worse than a beggar
seeking you.

I am not a saint,
nor am I a sinner,
and you are not
an angel, so come to me.
Come to me now,
while we are human.

# DID YOU THINK MY LOVE WAS FLEETING?

Did you think my love was fleeting?

I am not the dawn,
but the day that lasts.

When night arrives,
I increase to enfold you
in the peace of a thousand dreams.

Whether in dream or not –
last night, the future was pure sea
with great diamonds of light reflecting.
More than the surface of things,
my love penetrated into deep
water to be washed clean everlasting –

Now the essence of dear life
reflects my prayer.

Did you think my love was fleeting?

## NO SEPARATION

In the unfolding drama
of a rose's creation
sleeps no separation.
(It is where our souls meet.)
And beneath the searing torches
of your midnight petals, my spirit
sings with a virgin loveliness
as if I had never known life before.

*Lovers in Metamorphosis*

# SOMETIMES YOU ANSWER

Sometimes you answer me
as an ancient soul, familiar,
yet from a distance,
from the timeless

Sometimes you answer me
as an innocent youth,
an emerald reed just born
in the streams of time

Other times I see in your gaze
the infinite eyes of a wild creature
looking through and beyond me

You who come from other worlds,
how blessed that you visit
through the centuries
of your birthing deaths

Ever you bring a tenderness sublime,
the eternal gardens from which you sing

# SOFT LOVER OF DREAMS

And you roam in,
part stag, part human,
an unfallen Pan,
bringing the fountain
of an early spring rain

I wander to your glistening pools,
bending low, drinking of you,
of the pink rosebuds
of your fragrant glance

Within spring's approaching breath,
the meadow's invisible bud
adorns my hair,
wreathes my shoulders,
bejewels my breasts,
emerges through me

And you,
my dream of primal pollen,
feed my roots
with a rare essence, divine

The mossed branches
of my dryads' tree
let the acorns fall
as worlds we have borne,
without knowing

And then, as a walking tree
or visiting satyr,
you drift away and I am left
blossoming with freshly-spun jewels
embellishing my heart,
and wildflowers crowning my tresses

The wind howls, restless again,
whipping its flanks against
the rocky cliffs, wanting its own
soft lover of dreams

# THE FULL MOON'S WINE

With a hunger devouring me,
I stalk, like a white lioness
in the spell of the full moon's wine,
eyes glazed, drunk with the love of you

Root to root, paw to paw,
you infuse my circulation

The predator and the prey,
which is which?

With unseeing eyes,
the injured passion,
like an expectant beast,
lurks in the purple shadows,
awaiting the intoxication of you

# THE DRUMS OF THE EARTH'S PULSE

Reeling, swirling
as a flower so fragrant,
I am blown
by the winds of passion,
swept into forests
of flying root
Boughs reach out
in longing –

I whirl and spin,
brimming with the nectar
of you, my beloved

Is there a hesitancy
I am missing?
Is the thrust of passion
refusing stale restraint?

O my darling,
I thirst only for you,
the Sufi rhythm of you
dancing my heart
and beating the drums
of the earth's pulse
as our song

# I GROW BLOND WITH YOU

I grow blond with the meadows,
the grain caressed by the breeze,
the wild oats transparent
in the sun's rays

I grow blond with you
in my flaxen being
The earth, dry in the halcyon sun,
drinks of your protean soul

Where did you come from,
my dearest love?

Perhaps from the ageless forests
you've roamed,
riding the tender rays of dawns,
you've come

As the harbinger of early summer,
you bring the harvest of winter's frost

I grow blond with you
in my nakedness,
in my flaxen being
of this early summer,
bowing low in our dance of reverence

# OF THE LIZARD'S BREATH

We bathe in a shower
of golden beams

Garlands of flaming roses,
scarlet as your passion,
cascade upon my shoulders

Flaxen tresses
adorn the voluptuous hills
We imbibe summer's
warming breath,
renewed in God's heat

And in this
approaching summer,
we grow hair of gold,
green and red,
our wildflowers
again lost to seed

We know not
what will burgeon
in this scorch of sun,
in the dryness
of the lizard's breath

# OUR ETERNITY SHALL LIVE US

I drink of you, my beloved,
as the thirsty doe seeking the stream
in the dryness of late summer

I bathe in your luxury of bountiful heart
and walk your flanks –
reclining upon your chest

A strange, bittersweet sadness
creeps through me as I say goodnight

Our eternity shall live us, I vow,
and all else be shed
in sacrament to such grace

# A FLAWLESS ROSE OF DAWN

Just before the winter solstice,
just before a threatening winter,
you let flow from your being,
a golden seed,
a flawless rose of dawn,
a poem spilt from you
as pure as the streams
of tomorrow's storms,
vital as the thunder,
caressing as the softest feather

Above the crests of trees you soar
Your words uttered,
linger as rippling song notes
in cadence with the untamed gods
of the worlds beyond,
freeing the wingéd seed,
infusing mortal love
with the grandeur
of the white lion's prowl,
gilding the visiting angels' hearts
with the luminescence of a greater love

# MY LOVER, THE MOON

The ebony womb of night
is heavy with silent seed
Sentient trees stand witness
to all that can't be seen
Stars fall to the seas,
reflecting heaven's mystery

And I, swimming the black pools
of tomorrow's bloom,
await the moon's glimmering path

It arrives like my lover's message,
seducing me to drink of his breath,
the white vintage of his soul's beauty

I glide into his wavering arms,
lost in his sultry gaze,
becoming his, becoming different

In the drinking of each other,
we become One
Then he wanders on,
to love again in his resplendence

I will always wait for him,
for the moon of him,
in the seed of unknown tomorrows
I will always be his, reaching for him
as I swim his path of shimmering radiance

I am touched with the madness
                of becoming him

# REVEALS ETERNITY'S FACE

How may I look into eternity's eyes?
O God, tell me the way

How shall I touch eternity's lips?
O God, whisper the way

How shall I kiss eternity's face?
O God, please let me know

I greet you, O gallant soul,
as you arrive at my door
under the galaxy's dome
Bestowing your rose of fragrant spirit,
you embody immortality

For these moments you are love
in the clothes of a man,
but the radiance you cast,
reveals eternity's face

# OF AN INTIMATE DISTANCE

Enlustered by
the umbral cloak of night,
you lean over me,
eyes brimming with stars

As a wild creature
shimmering in moonbeams,
you hover

And the dark's secrets
swim within us,
taking us on travels
of lost light,
shadows of ghosts,
auras of the future

We are held beyond
and within the seamless depths
of an intimate distance

# OF CONSTELLATIONS UNFORMED

You leave paths
of lush, red roses blooming
on this winter's eve

Pollen-fragranced,
these fields of red stars
incense me from within

And what else do you leave behind
for the creatures wandering
the nocturnal shadows?
What else, tender one,
do you leave for us?

Is it you who has gathered
the fallen stars to light my way?

Is it you who enters
my midnight and curls up there,
holding me infinitely in your arms?

You rest now, sleeping,
and your dreams breathe me
into another chamber,
into a radiant darkness
of constellations unformed

# QUIESCENT AFTER THE STORM

Tonight you return to me,
like the solstice of the winter sun
turning toward the light

We had become each other's ashes,
carcasses of past orgies,
now left in abandonment
to the ruthless beasts of Nature's change

The unmerciful face of a dark god
had watched us blaze,
turn to cinders in each other's arms

But now, for this abundant moment,
we glow as One
in the ebony kingdom of night

We rest upon a meadow of pink sheets,
warm, filled with our pomegranate wine
Below, the tides resound,
quiescent after the storm,
as we, for the moment, can be

*Untitled*

# VISIONS OF GLORY

Oh delicate balance
on whose perilous edge
life thrives.

Poets dwell there, too.

But look at the lovers
perched atop that precarious
precipice of ecstasy,

As delicately as dawn
walks over the horizon.

# FOR CAROLYN

Like a plant
whose roots are infinite,
you grow in me.

Like a star
whose light is human,
you shine in me.

Like a sky
that has grown arms,
you hold me.

Like a bird
whose wings
have become a heart,
you love me.

# SHALL I TREMBLE

Shall I tremble
infinitely when you
place your hands
upon me?

And what flames
flashing lie waiting
in your feminine fingers,
make my phoenix rise?

Oh are you the bird
of my dreams soaring?

Or are you
the whole sky
the image of my love
takes flight in?

# I STILL LOVE YOU

Take it all away;
I still love you.

Leave empty my hands
for I must lose;
I still love you.

Take it all away, leave me
naked and nameless
under infinite sky;
I still love you.

## PLANTED WITHIN

If I am the seed
then thou art the rose
that bears me.

Unfold yourself,
petal by petal
until your soul
stands naked –

I will be there,
planted within,
as in the gardens
of eternity.

## LAST NIGHT

Last night, my lover died in my
arms and her soft flesh sunk
into my chest.

Like a good poet, I let her go,
opened my heart and
watched her go tumbling through the
door to the dark roots of things.

It was there, in the breathless
garden of my love,
I set her free.

# ABOUT THE AUTHORS

CAROLYN MARY KLEEFELD was born in Catford, England and grew up in southern California where she studied art and psychology at UCLA. In 1980, she moved to her cliff-side home high above the Pacific Ocean in Big Sur, California, where she studies, writes, and paints amidst the wilderness around her.

With a passion for creative expression and a lifelong fascination with spiritual transformation, she is an award-winning poet and artist, whose books have been used as inspirational texts in universities worldwide, and translated into Braille by the Library of Congress. Her art has been featured in galleries and museums nationwide.

*Web:*      *www.carolynmarykleefeld.com*
*Email:*    *info@carolynmarykleefeld.com*

*Telephone: (800) 403-3635 or (831) 667-2433*
*Address:   PO Box 370, Big Sur, California 93920*

DAVID WAYNE DUNN was born in Fresno, California where he lived before making his home in Big Sur in 1997. Moved by existence, he began writing poetry in his late teens while reading such authors as Robinson Jeffers and DH Lawrence.

In addition to exhibiting his artwork, David has participated in numerous poetry readings. He can be heard wandering the woods, singing to the wind – and often reciting poetry in nearby coffee houses accompanying himself on the guitar and harmonica.

He is currently working on a book of poetry and prose titled *The Naked Death of a Lover.*

*Email:*     *ddunn3@earthlink.net*
*Telephone: (831) 667-2223*
*Address:    PO Box 96, Big Sur, California 93920*

# BOOKS BY CAROLYN KLEEFELD

*The Alchemy of Possibility: Reinventing Your Personal Mythology*
with Foreword by Laura Huxley *(can be used as an oracle and
includes prose, poetry, and paintings, as well as quotes from the Tarot
and I Ching)*
MERRILL-WEST PUBLISHING, CARMEL, CA 1998

*Songs of Ecstasy, Limited Edition (poetry)*
ATOMS MIRROR ATOMS, INC, CARMEL, CA 1990 *(out of print)*

*Songs of Ecstasy*
*(art booklet commemorating Carolyn's 1990 solo exhibition)*
ATOMS MIRROR ATOMS, INC, CARMEL, CA 1990

*Lovers in Evolution*
*(includes poetry and Palomar Observatory photographs)*
THE HORSE & BIRD PRESS, LOS ANGELES, CA 1983

*Satan Sleeps with the Holy: Word Paintings (poetry)*
THE HORSE & BIRD PRESS, LOS ANGELES, CA 1982

*Climates of the Mind (includes poetry and sayings)*
THE HORSE & BIRD PRESS, LOS ANGELES, CA 1979 *(in 3rd printing)*

Carolyn is interviewed along with Allen Ginsberg, Terence
McKenna, Timothy Leary, Laura Huxley, and others in: *Mavericks
of the Mind: Conversations for the New Millennium* by David Jay
Brown & Rebecca Novick.
THE CROSSING PRESS, FREEDOM, CA 1993

Carolyn has completed a manuscript of poetry titled *Pagan Love
Poems for Living and Dying*, is preparing a book of her sayings for
publication, and is completing a book of her fables, titled *The Last
Voice of a Human Dinosaur.*

For more information, contact:

*Atoms Mirror Atoms, Inc.*
*Address:    PO Box 221693 Carmel, California 93922*
*Telephone: (800) 403-3635 or (831) 667-2433*
*Web:       www.carolynmarykleefeld.com*